PENGUIN BOOKS

DEAR KATIE

Jacky Fleming went to a suffragette s[...] emerged awesomely uneducated due to the teachers' inexplicable preference for Latin as a first language. A year at Chelsea School of Art and a degree in fine art at Leeds University greatly improved her table football technique. Other qualifications include A– for posture and a silver medal in Latin-American dancing. A brief stint in the art department of a London periodical was followed by eleven years teaching art as a foreign language. Jacky lives in Yorkshire and hates cooking.

Her cartoons have been published by (among others) the BBC, The Women's Press, Virago, Leeds Postcards, The Open University, *Independent on Sunday*, *New Stateman & Society*, *New Internationalist* and *New Woman*. Penguin also publish her popular books of cartoons, *Be a Bloody Train Driver!*, *Never Give Up* and *Falling in Love*.

JACKY FLEMING

Dear Katie

AUGUST 1/98.

DEAR KATHRYN ANNE,

HERE'S A FUNNY LITTLE BOOK
I THOUGHT YOU MIGHT LIKE TO MAKE
YOU SMILE. IT'S BEEN A WHILE SINCE
I BOUGHT YOU ANYTHING FOR YOUR
BIRTHDAY. I WASN'T QUITE SURE
WHAT TO GET. YOU ARE NOT AN EASY
PERSON TO FIND A GIFT FOR. SO HERE

PENGUIN BOOKS

IT IS, BECAUSE LAUGHTER MAKES LIFE
BETTER. AND ON YOUR 21ST BIRTHDAY I
HOPE LIFE JUST GETS BETTER AND BETTER!
LOVE EMMA

PENGUIN BOOKS

Published by the Penguin Group
Penguin Books Ltd, 27 Wrights Lane, London W8 5TZ, England
Penguin Books USA Inc., 375 Hudson Street, New York, New York 10014, USA
Penguin Books Australia Ltd, Ringwood, Victoria, Australia
Penguin Books Canada Ltd, 10 Alcorn Avenue, Toronto, Ontario, Canada M4V 3B2
Penguin Books (NZ) Ltd, 182–190 Wairau Road, Auckland 10, New Zealand

Penguin Books Ltd, Registered Offices: Harmondsworth, Middlesex, England

First published in Penguin Books 1994
1 3 5 7 9 10 8 6 4 2

This book is dedicated to those bewildered men
who have provided such a fruitful source
of inspiration, and without whom this book
would not have been necessary.

Dear Katie,
Am I the only man who's
totally confused by feminism?
I can't seem to open my
mouth these days without
someone flying off the handle.

Give us a break girls!

Dear Dave,

I've had so many letters like yours.
You men really are getting the brunt
of it, aren't you. Bear with them, it's
probably just the time of the month.

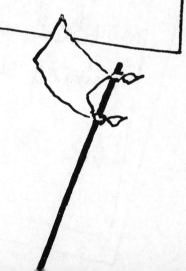

Dear Katie,

Since I was a teenager I've smoked to stay thin, but increasingly it seems a terrible price to pay. What will be the point of being slim if I'm dead?

Dear Joyce,

What's the point in being alive
if you're dumpy? We all have to
compromise to stay attractive.

Dear Katie,
I've noticed with horror the first signs of cellulite on my behind. Short of liposuction what can I do about it?

Dear Judy,

Face forward at all times when unclothed. Practise leaving the room backwards in a casual manner. Don't despair – some women have been doing it for years.

Dear Katie,
After twelve years of marriage I thought our sex life needed perking up a bit and bought my wife some (expensive) erotic underwear. She tried it on once to please me but has refused to wear it again. How can I persuade her that she looks terrific in it?

Dear Damion,

How thoughtful of you. Buy a
soft-porn magazine, available
at any respectable newsagent,
and tell her she looks just as
good as the real thing. I'm
sure she'll feel flattered.

Dear Katie,

I think my husband may be having an affair. He's very late home looking sheepish and unnaturally tidy. He smells faintly of perfume, is embarrassingly jovial, and obsequiously helpful over the most trivial things.

If he starts bringing me little presents I may kill him.

Dear Jane,

Enjoy it while it lasts. He'll be
morose and uncooperative again in
no time.

Dear Katie,
I'm a male student and I go to lots of parties. The trouble is I don't know what's allowed these days and what isn't. You've only got to look at someone to end up in court. What am I supposed to do?

Dear Katie,

My new partner is very reluctant to use condoms. I think it's a small thing to ask considering the risks, but he goes into a sulk if I even mention it. I'm afraid if I make a fuss he'll find someone else.

Dear Pat,

Do you want to keep him, or to lose him? That is the real risk. Perhaps you don't really love him.

Dear Katie,
My husband recently left me
and our three young children
to live with one of his students.
He says he no longer finds me
attractive because I'm always
tired, and don't 'make an effort'
any more.

Dear Jill,

How disheartening for your husband to watch you turn into a drudge. Too many women become immersed in themselves and take their husbands for granted. No wonder they seek solace elsewhere.

Dear Katie,

Everywhere I look women seem to be in a state of perpetual disappointment with men. Is this because they expect too much of us, or because we really are so horrible?

Dear Peter,

Both. Women still believe that
beneath a veneer of uncompromising
self-interest lies a loyal and
compassionate man.

Dear Katie,

If I ask my partner to clean up after himself he looks contrite and says he'll do it later. If I ask again he mutters about 'nagging'. If I ask again he's downright hostile, shouts 'I said I'd do it', but he still doesn't.

Is this why women end up doing it after all?

Dear Pam,

It's not really worth falling out about, is it? He probably thinks it's easier for you because you know where things are kept.

Dear Katie,

Sometimes my husband gets drunk and becomes aggressive. Last week he kicked the cat. Most of the time he's an easy going sort of man. Am I doing something to upset him?

Dear Janice,

Probably. Perhaps you've been wearing a colour he doesn't like. Try to find out what he does like and keep to it. Some men are very sensitive.

Dear Katie,
Why is it always men who
are accused of domestic
violence? Only the other day
I read an article about a
woman who was violent
towards her husband, so why
are we always the guilty party?
It makes me so angry . .

Dear Steve,

I have to admit I missed the article
you mention, but it does rather change
our understanding of domestic violence.
Thank-you for pointing it out.

Dear Katie,

For twelve years I lived with a man who did nothing but undermine my confidence in every way. He convinced me that I was worthless, which made it even more difficult to muster the resources to leave. I did finally leave a year ago and can't believe how much better I feel.

I just can't understand why he did it.

Dear Claire,

Men and their little ways!
He did it to keep you there.
It worked did it not?

Dear Katie,
Why do businessmen take their clients to strip-clubs? They pretend it's for the 'friendly ambience' but I can't see what's friendly about paying someone to take their clothes off and move in the most ridiculous way. Don't men object to seeing women humiliate themselves for money?

Dear Katie,

I have a wonderful career which I enjoy immensely. Due to recent promotion I earn a higher salary than my husband.

We have a good marriage but he is reacting badly to the difference in our wages.

Dear Katie,

I'd describe myself as a non-sexist liberal man, and I fully approve of my wife's career. The problem arises after work.

She insists that we share the chores and childcare, but quite honestly, after a hard day's work it's the last thing I want to do.

Dear Paul,

It's a crying shame but a lot of young women these days are neglecting their parental and family duties. Why don't you offer to help out - make her a cup of tea when she gets in. It could make all the difference.

Dear Katie,
What is it with women these days? I, for one, appreciate an attractive pair of legs, and I know a lot of other men would agree with me. Don't they like to be admired any more?

Dear Brian,

I ask myself the same question.
A quick flick with the ladyshave
and a slight chill seems a very
small price to pay for such a high
reward.

Dear Katie,

I am sick to the back teeth of films which eroticise the terror of a woman being pursued by a violent predatory man. It seems to be the staple theme of the film industry. Surely it indicates something profoundly amiss with our culture.

Dear Julia,

Don't be so melodramatic.
Celluloid fantasies have nothing
to do with real life. Do grow up.

Dear Katie,
I've just finished reading
'Dirty Weekend' and all I
can say is the writer is
a sick woman.

Dear Mike,

I agree there is something
unnatural about it. Sadism
in a woman is so unattractive.

Dear Katie,
I know my husband prefers
large breasts, and mine are
on the small side.
Should I consider cosmetic
surgery?

Dear Carol,

Obviously, or he may run off with a larger breasted woman, and who could blame him?

A word of warning though - you may lose all sensation in your nipples, but I'm sure he's worth it.

Dear Katie,

I want both my teenage sons to grow up into caring sensitive men but I have to say I see no signs of this happening. What amazes me is that there seems to be no shortage of terrific girlfriends who find the sullen, slovenly ineptitude of my sons irresistible.

Is there no hope?

Dear Fran,

None whatsoever.

Dear Katie,

I'm outraged that after working for the same company for eight years, I've been sacked because I'm expecting a child. My boss has children, and a wife to look after them. Why is it built into our institutions that men are not required to take care of their children?

Dear Sandra,

Men are too busy.

Dear Katie,

Why is it that just because I don't want children enough to actually HAVE any, I'm regarded either as a child-hater, or too immature to be a responsible parent, or someone whose experience of life is pathetically incomplete?

Dear Liz,

Clearly you are not yet ready for the challenges and incomparable rewards of motherhood. In the meantime I'm sure you can find useful ways of keeping yourself occupied.

Dear Katie,
For some reason nobody has
ever sent me a Valentine.
Until now I haven't given it a
second thought, but if I don't
get one this year I think I'll
be a bit disappointed.

Do you think it's worth
worrying about?

Dear Donna,

Yes I do. People obviously don't
find you attractive. Try wearing
pink more often and flirt a bit.
Too late for this year, probably.

Dear Katie,

I've always been good academically, but now I'm worried that it puts boys off. I have two degrees, one in Physics, and one in Pure Maths.

Should I play it down?

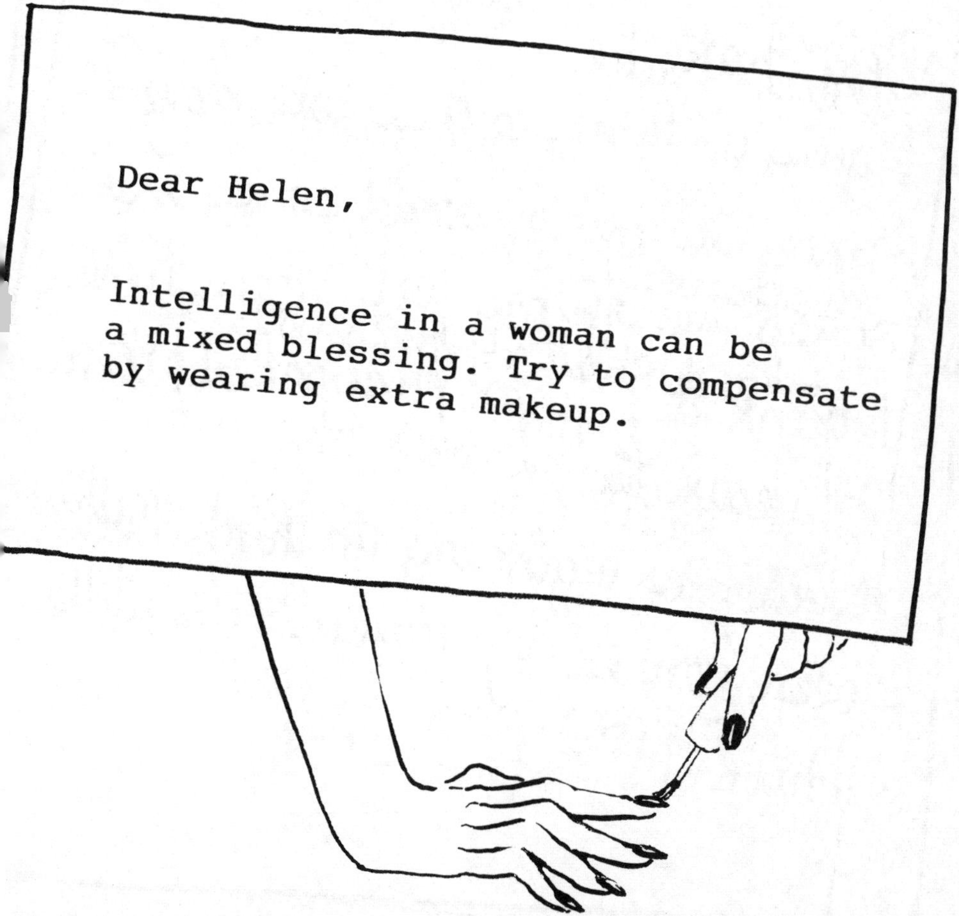
Dear Helen,
Intelligence in a woman can be a mixed blessing. Try to compensate by wearing extra makeup.

Dear Katie,

I grew up thinking that one day Prince Charming would come and sweep me off my feet. Each time I think it's finally happened, then it wears off.

Now I'm beginning to think I've been conned by romantic twaddle.

Have I?

Dear Katie,

I'm caught in a Catch 22 situation. If I disagree with anything my husband says he accuses me of nagging. Sometimes I hardly dare speak. It leaves me unable to communicate with him, and leaves him free to do whatever he wants. How can I break this deadlock so that I can have a say as well?

Dear Katie,

I've tried anti-ageing creams but they don't seem to make any difference to my face.

Can you suggest any alternatives?

Dear Cath,

You're right. The creams don't work. Try to keep your face completely expressionless at all times. Avoid frowning or smiling if you can.

Dear Katie,

I seem to have more body hair than other women and even the occasional hair on my face.

Is this normal?

Dear Sheila,

Yes, it is perfectly normal, but
thanks to electrolysis, depilatory
creams, waxing, plucking, and the
good old razor it's a well kept secret.
Please don't spoil it for the rest of
us by letting the cat out of the bag.

Dear Katie,

Why do I keep hearing about families needing the security and stability of a responsible father, when most single mothers have left, or been left by, an irresponsible one?

Dear Katie,

Since the birth of my baby I've been terribly depressed. I feel trapped and isolated at home, and I miss the stimulus of my job and going out. The biggest shock has been that I have no maternal instincts and feel the responsibility for my baby's well-being and safety as a terrifying burden. What makes it even worse is that I'm perpetually exhausted from lack of sleep.

Dear Mary,

Buck up.

Dear Katie,

My children are at that age where they are obsessed with sweets. When we go to buy some we are confronted by a shelf of magazines displaying photos of naked women in the most absurd and humiliating poses. I can't help wondering what effect this may have on my children's future attitudes.

Dear Alison,

It surprises me that you allow your children to eat sweets, which, unlike pornography, are known to be harmful.

Dear Katie,

I don't want to sound petty but it does rile me that my female friends can lech unrepentantly over some tall dark rippling hunk, while if I so much as look at another woman I'm living on borrowed time.

I'm sorry but I don't think it's fair.

Dear Nick,

Don't be sorry - this is a
serious matter. I'm sure you
are tall dark and rippling
in your own way. Women can
be so insensitive.

Dear Katie,

Who buys all that gorgeous underwear I see in the shops? It certainly isn't me, and if it's any of my friends they haven't owned up.

Is everyone having a wildly depraved and exciting time except me?

Dear Melanie,

Yes.

Dear Katie,
Everyone says that size
doesn't matter - it's what he
does with it that counts.
But I can't entirely agree.

Am I being sexist?

Dear Ros,

Yes.
How would you like it if men
talked about us like that?

Dear Katie,

How exactly do you get the duvet cover back on?

Dear Bob,

Are you single, dear? The usual
solution is to move in with a nice
girlfriend who does it for you.

Dear Katie,
Why is it that even in these days of so-called equality, women's magazines are still almost entirely about how to make yourself as attractive and desirable as you can?

Dear Sarah,

Why do you think feminism flopped?
Liberation in the nineties is about
the right to look good and feel sexy.
Am I right, girls?